To Root, to Toot, to Parachute

What Is a Verb?

To Mary Kate, Jack, and Colin—
three "action" kids   —B.P.C.

To my sister, Margarita
—J.P.

Verb: **A word that shows action or being.**

To Root, to Toot, to Parachute

What Is a Verb?

by Brian P. Cleary

illustrated by Jenya Prosmitsky

CAROLRHODA BOOKS, INC. / MINNEAPOLIS

Whether you **scale** a Wall or a fish,

Make a design on a cup or a dish,

To root,
to
toot,

to
parachute,

To play the
flutophone or
flute,

Verbs are words like sing and dance,

Pray or practice,

preach or prance,

So are holler, help, and hold,

Whack and stack and pack and fold,

Fix and *finish*,

load and **lift**,

Hurry, Scurry, Shake, and **sift**.

So take a present,

Send your thanks,

Pull a tooth, or pull some pranks,

Blow a bubble,

Sew a sleeve,

You'll use a **Verb** for each of these.

That is fun,

It's been great,

Were you the one who was so late?

Punt or pass or shoot or score,

swim or paddle, pitch or pour,

Jog
or
juggle,

jig or leap,

Verbs can tire
you out a heap.

So pick and fiddle, strum and stroke,

Tease and teeter,

Sob and soak,

Have and has belong here too,

Like

"I have green eyes,

She has blue."

Or "Mindy **has** a
mini mutt."

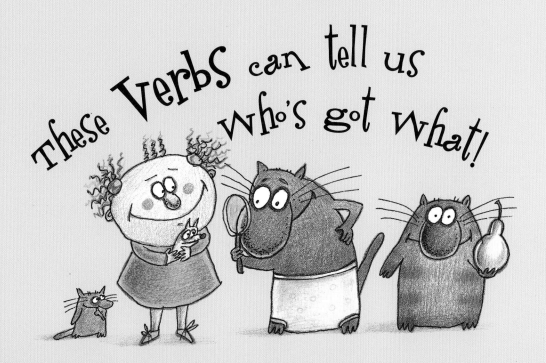

These **Verbs** can tell us
who's got what!

They tell us of dogs
that are **barking** or sleeping,

BEEP
BEEP

of cars that are **racing**,
or merely **beep-beeping**,

Of planes that are *flying*,

and trains choo-choo-chooing,

Aunt Edna "Oh-Hi-ing,"

and Mom "Toodle-ooing"—

So, whether it's
dangerous,
dull, or superb,

Each sentence, you see,
simply must have a **Verb!**

VERB POWER

VERBS ARE COOL

ABOUT THE AUTHOR & ILLUSTRATOR

BRIAN P. CLEARY is the author of several other picture books, including A Mink, a Fink, a Skating Rink: What Is a Noun? and Hairy, Scary, Ordinary: What Is an Adjective? He lives in Cleveland, Ohio.

JENYA PROSMITSKY grew up and studied art in Chisinau, Moldova, and lives in Minneapolis. Her two cats, Henry and Freddy, were vital to her illustrations for this book and the other Words Are Categorical books.

This book is available in two editions:
Library binding by Carolrhoda Books, Inc., a division of Lerner Publishing Group
Soft cover by First Avenue Editions, an imprint of Lerner Publishing Group
241 First Avenue North, Minneapolis, MN 55401 U.S.A.

Website address: www.lernerbooks.com

Library of Congress Cataloging-in-Publication Data

Cleary, Brian P., 1959-
   To root, to toot, to parachute : what is verb? / by Brian P. Cleary ; illustrated by Jenya Prosmitsky.
      p. cm. — (Words are categorical)
   Summary: Rhyming text and illustrations of comical cats present numerous examples of verbs, from "toss and tumble," "jump and jam," to "whine and whimper," "sleep and slam."
   ISBN 1-57505-403-5 (lib. bdg. : alk. paper)
   ISBN 1-57505-418-3 (pbk. : alk. paper)
   1. English language—Verb—Juvenile literature. [1. English language—Verb.]
I. Prosmitsky, Jenya, 1974- ill. II. Title. III. Series: Cleary, Brian P., 1959-
Words are categorical.
PE1271.C58 1999   98-49569
428.2—dc21

Manufactured in the United States of America
5 6 7 8 9 10 - JR - 07 06 05 04 03 01